GREAT PIANO SOLOS

Wise Publications
London/New York/Paris/Sydney/Copenhagen/Berlin/Madrid/Tokyo

Exclusive Distributors:
Music Sales Limited
14/15 Berners Street,
London W1T 3LJ, England.

Music Sales Pty Limited
120 Rothschild Avenue,
Rosebery, NSW 2018,
Australia.

Order No. AM89684
ISBN 0-7119-3055-4
This book © Copyright 2004 by Wise Publications.

'Crazy' and 'Wade In The Water' arranged by Jack Long.
'Beyond The Sea', 'Don't Know Why', 'Hallelujah I Love Her So',
'I Wanna Be Loved By You' and 'So What' arranged by Quentin Thomas.

Your Guarantee of Quality:
As publishers, we strive to produce every book to the highest commercial
standards. This book has been carefully designed to minimise awkward
page turns and to make playing from it a real pleasure. Particular care has
been given to specifying acid-free, neutral-sized paper made from pulps
which have not been elemental chlorine bleached. This pulp is from farmed
sustainable forests and was produced with special regard for the
environment. Throughout, the printing and binding have been planned to
ensure a sturdy, attractive publication which should give years of
enjoyment. If your copy fails to meet our high standards, please inform us
and we will gladly replace it.

www.musicsales.com

CONTENTS

The Arrival Of The Queen Of Sheba

Music by George Frideric Handel

Canon in D

Music by Johann Pachelbel

9

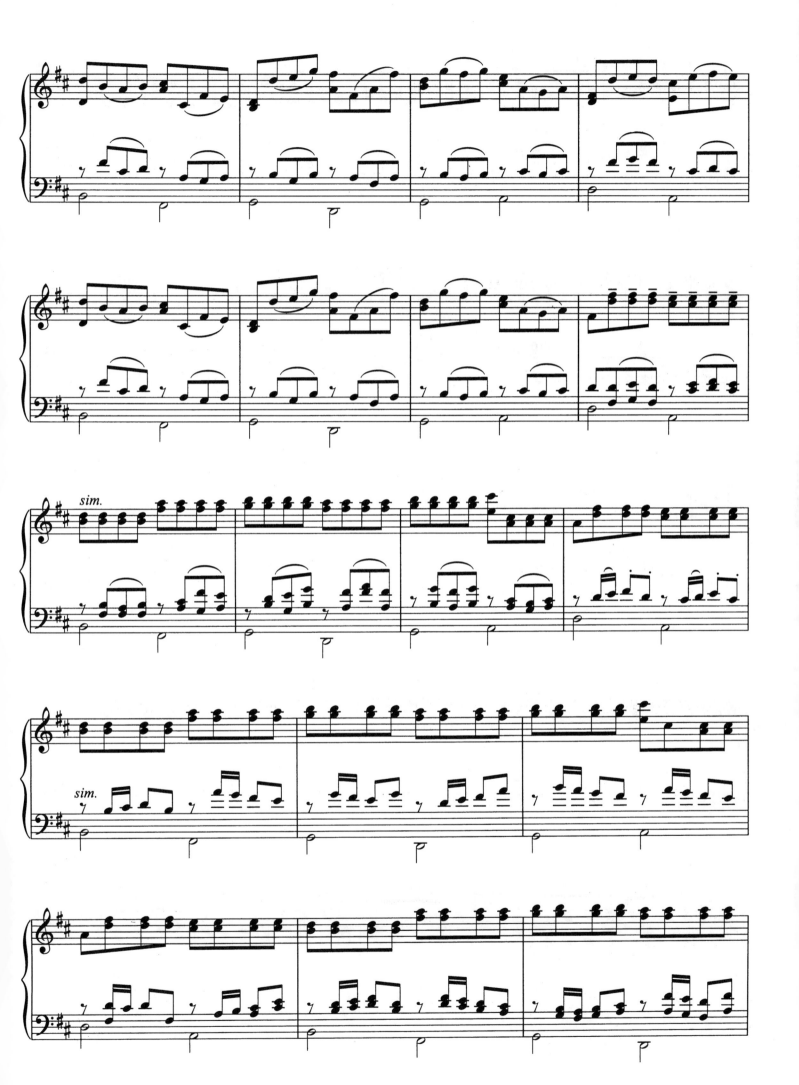

1812 Overture

Music by Peter Ilyich Tchaikovsky

Largo (♩ = 60)

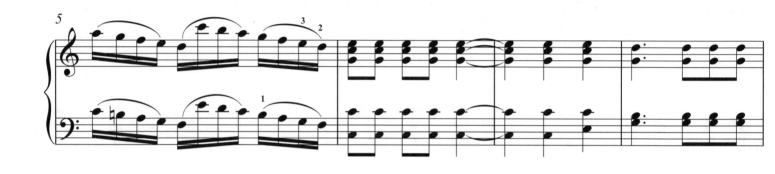

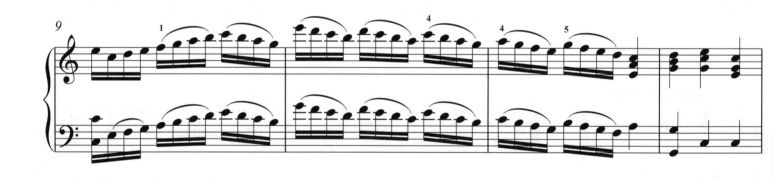

In The Hall Of The Mountain King

Music by Edvard Grieg

Alla marcia e molto marcato (♩ = 138)

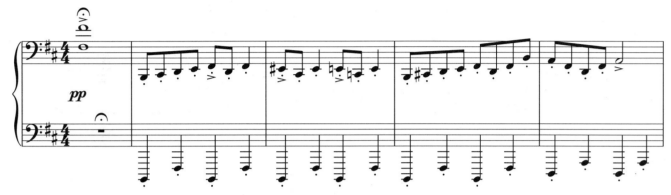

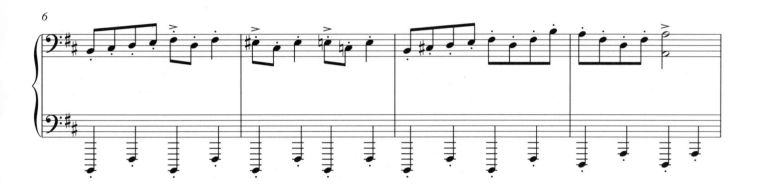

poco a poco cresc. e stretto

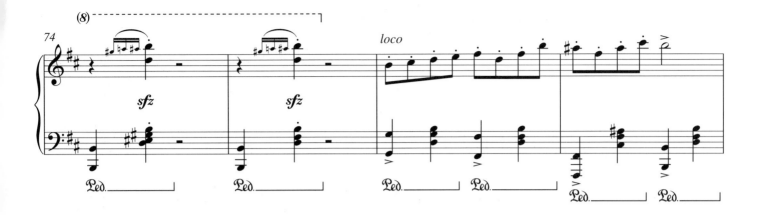

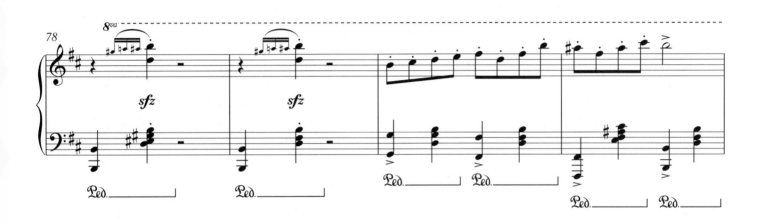

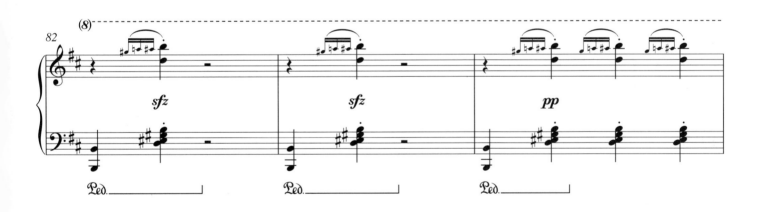

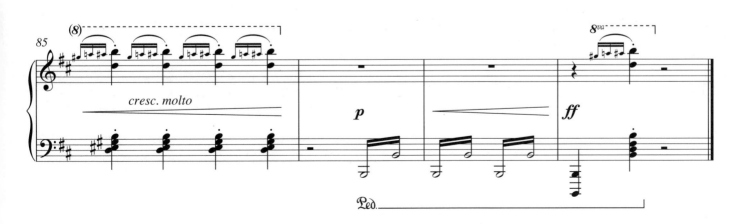

Jesu, Joy Of Man's Desiring

Music by Johann Sebastian Bach

rall. poco a poco

25

Nocturne in E♭ Major Op.9, No.2

Music by Frédéric Chopin

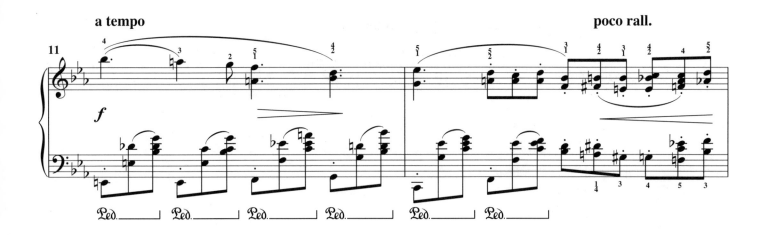

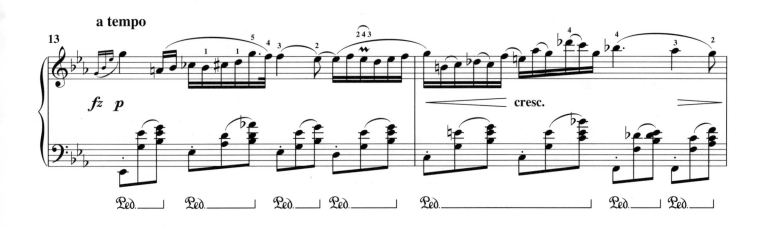

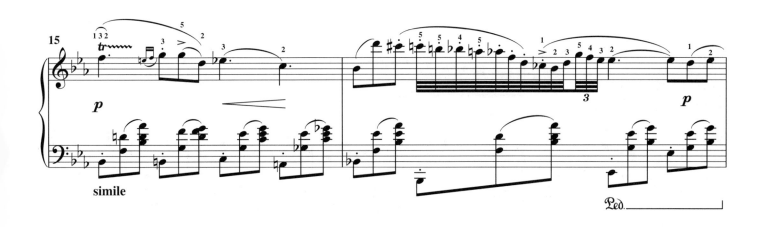

poco rall.　　　　　　　　a tempo

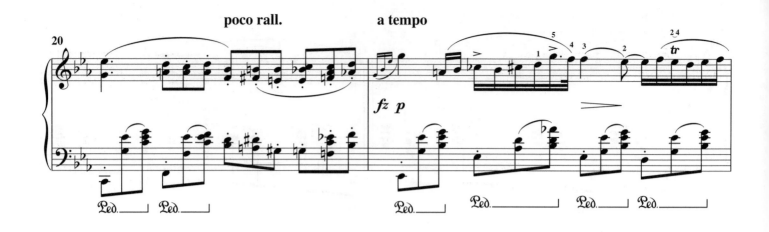

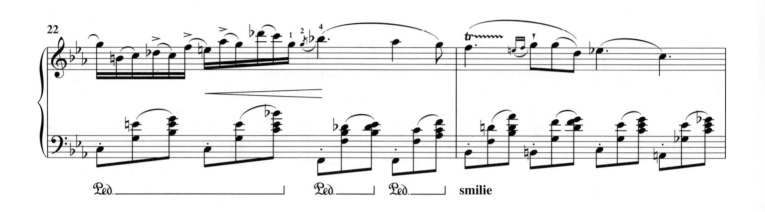

smilie

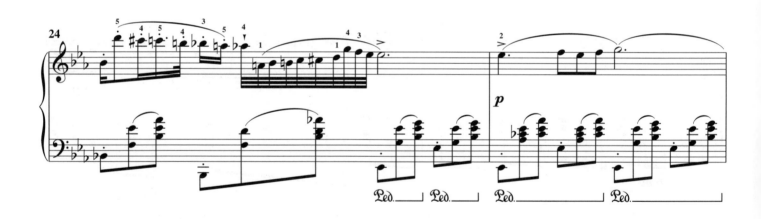

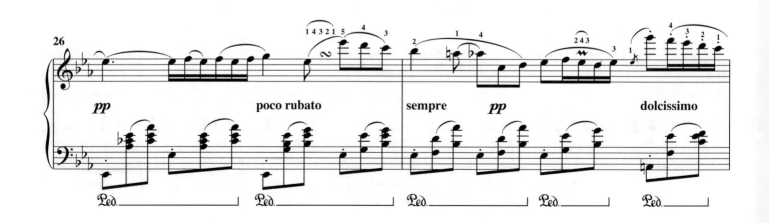

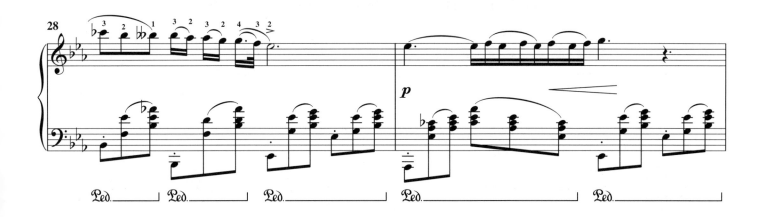

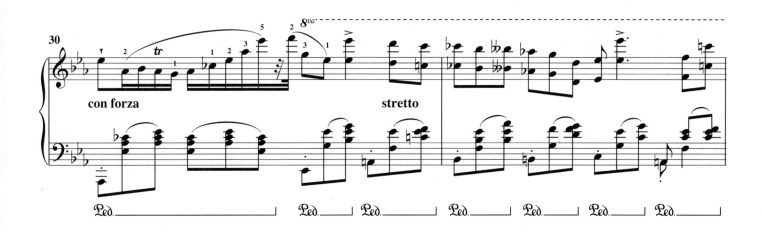

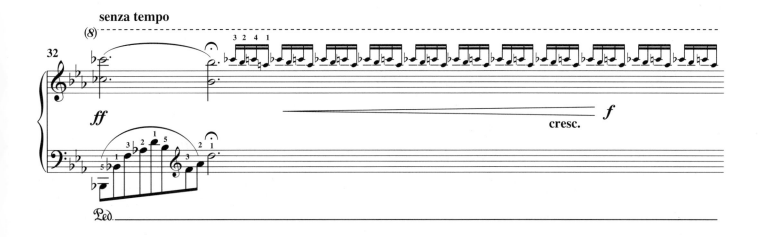

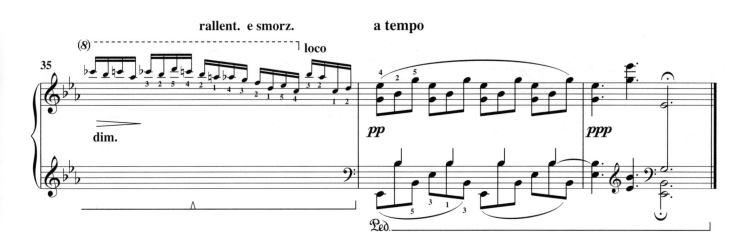

The Ride Of The Valkyries

Music by Richard Wagner

31

Symphony No.5, Adagietto: 4th Movement

Music by Gustav Mahler

poco a poco cresc.

ff

Ped.

dim.

3
3

p

rit.

pp

35

After Midnight
(from the film "Chicago")

Music by Danny Elfman

38

The Last Of The Mohicans
(Main Theme)

Music by Trevor Jones

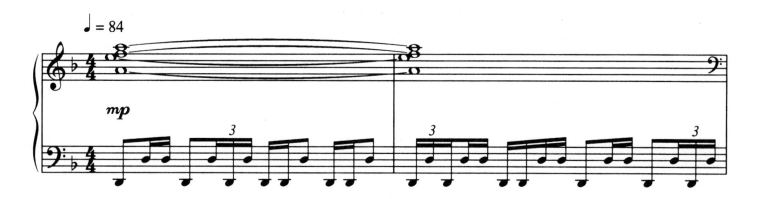

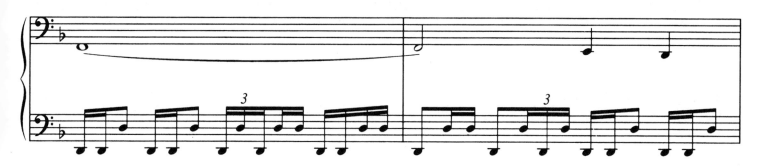

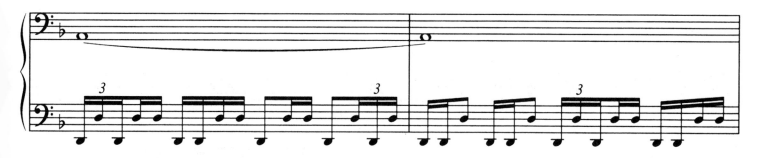

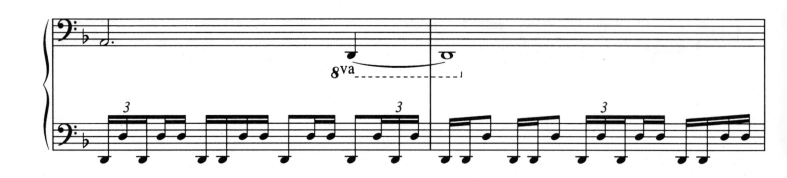

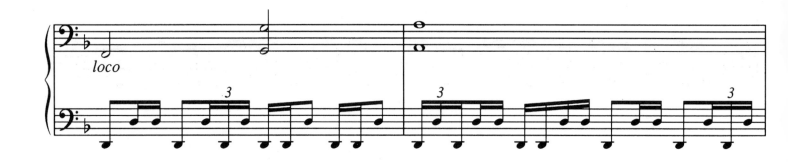

Honor Him/Now We Are Free
(from the film "Gladiator")

Music by Hans Zimmer, Lisa Gerrard & Klaus Badelt

I. HONOR HIM

poco accel.

$\flat$ = $\downarrow$ = 140

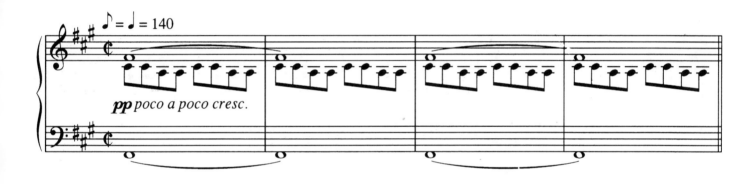

II. NOW WE ARE FREE

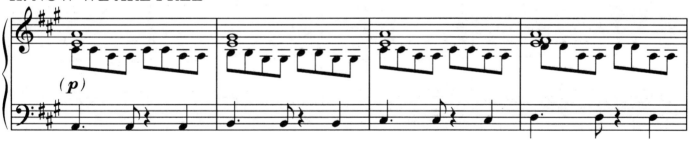

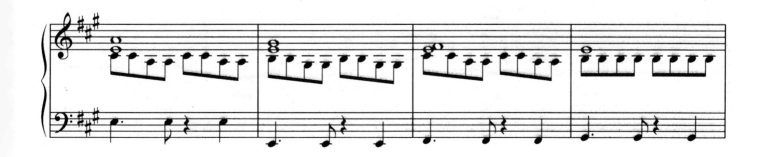

Slower, freely

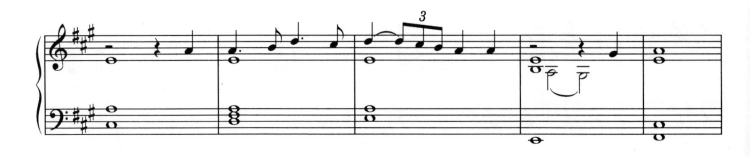

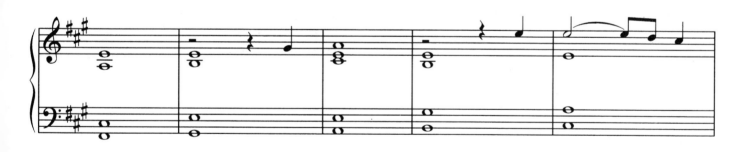

rit.

poco dim.

Glasgow Love Theme
(from the film "Love Actually")

Words & Music by Craig Armstrong

Slowly, very freely

Big My Secret
(from the film "The Piano")

Music by Michael Nyman

I Wanna Be Loved By You
(from the film "Some Like It Hot")

Words by Bert Kalmar
Music by Herbert Stothart & Harry Ruby

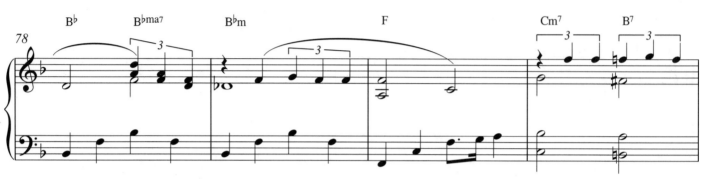

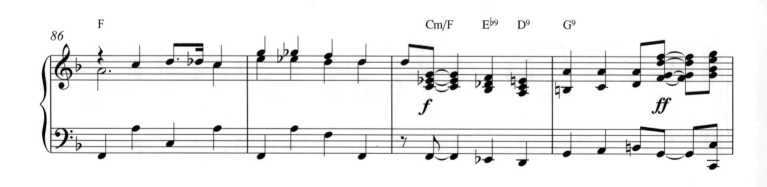

My Heart Will Go On
(Love Theme From "Titanic")

Words by Will Jennings
Music by James Horner

67

Beyond The Sea

Original words & music by Charles Trenet

English words by Jack Lawrence

Both Sides, Now

Words & Music by Joni Mitchell

73

Crazy

Words & Music by Willie Nelson

Here, There And Everywhere

Words & Music by John Lennon & Paul McCartney

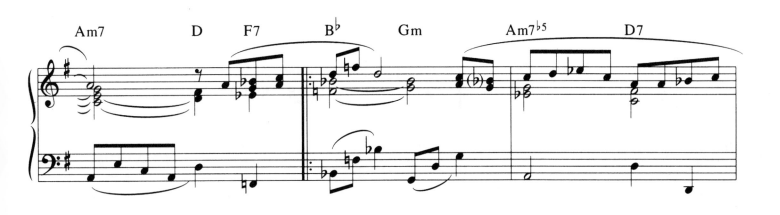

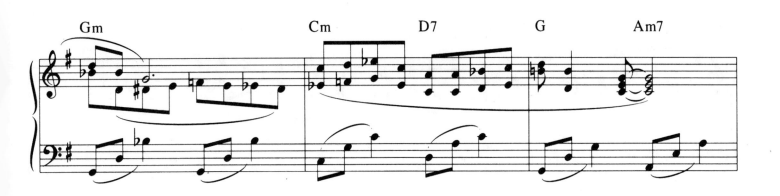

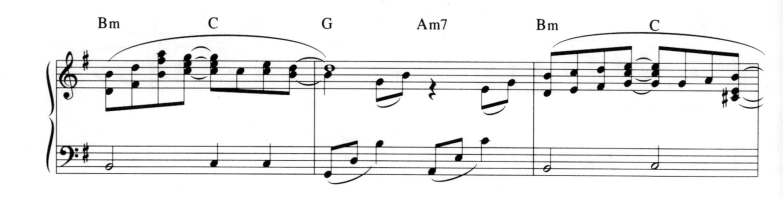

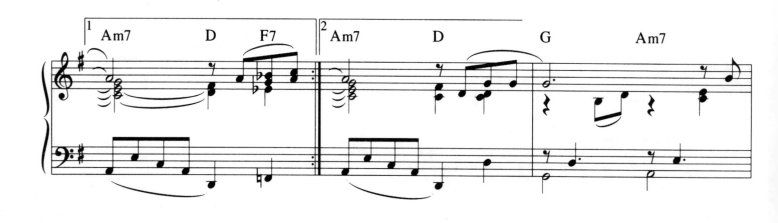

I Say A Little Prayer

Words by Hal David
Music by Burt Bacharach

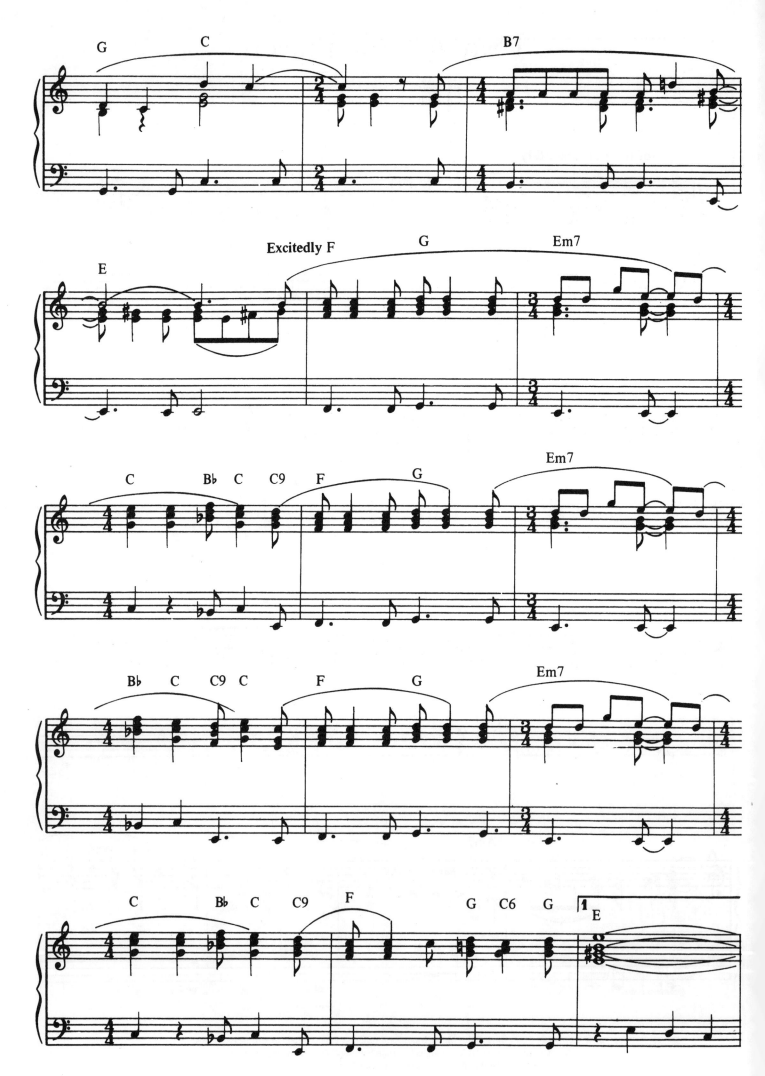

Killing Me Softly With His Song

Words by Norman Gimbel
Music by Charles Fox

Rocket Man

Words & Music by Elton John & Bernie Taupin

Moderately slow, with a beat

87

REPEAT AND FADE

90

Still Crazy After All These Years

Words & Music by Paul Simon

Caravan

Words & Music by Duke Ellington, Irving Mills & Juan Tizol

Moderato Quasi Misterioso

Misterioso

98

Hallelujah I Love Her So

Words & Music by Ray Charles

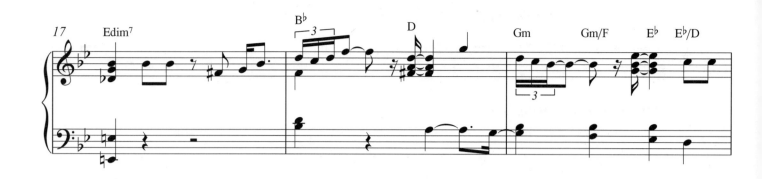

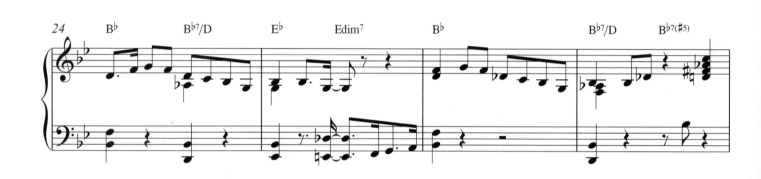

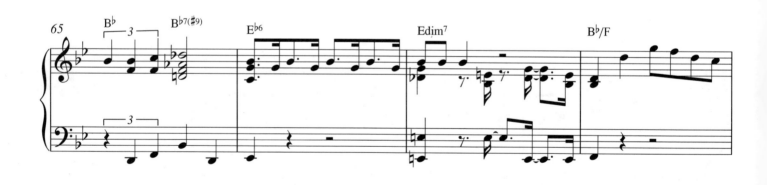

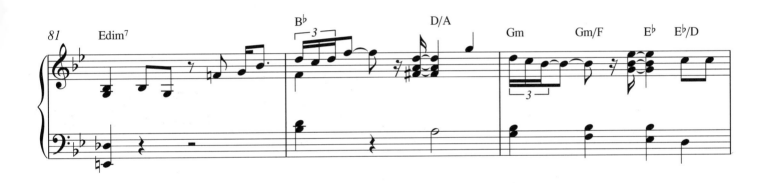

Don't Know Why

Words & Music by Jesse Harris

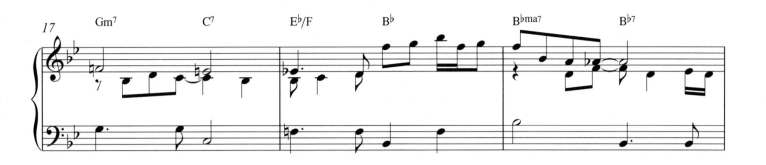

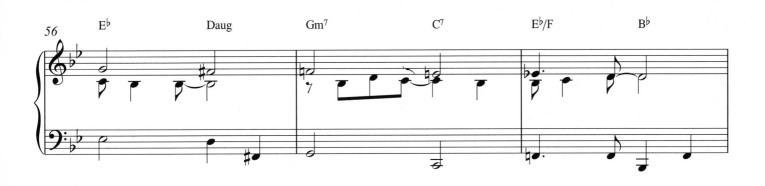

poco rall.

The Lady Sings The Blues

Words by Billie Holiday
Music by Herbie Nichols

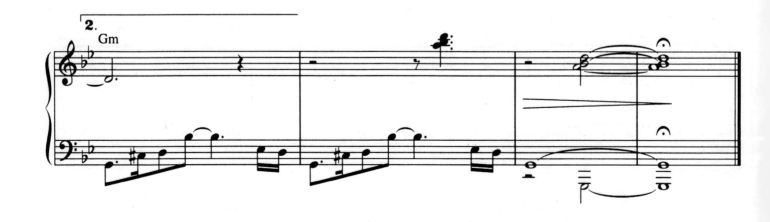

Misty

Music by Erroll Garner

Slowly, with expression

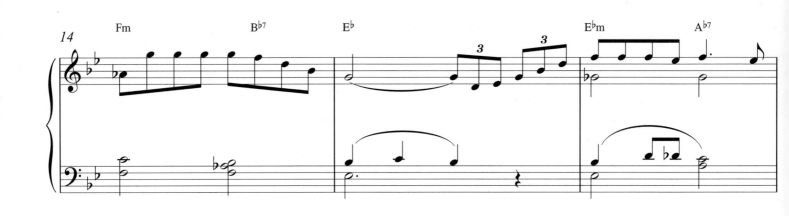

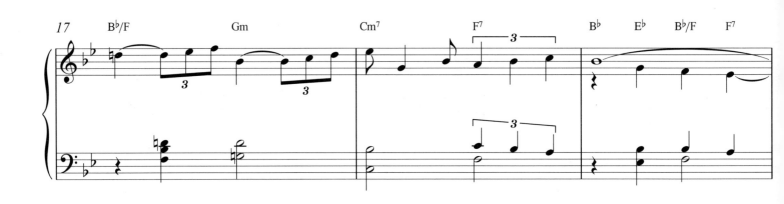

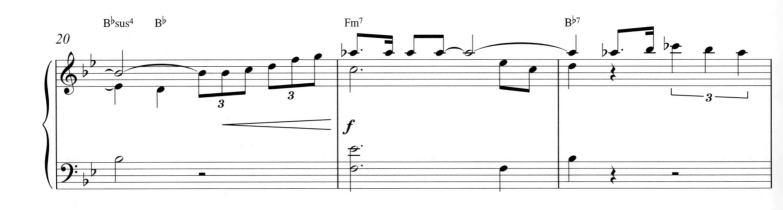

Maple Leaf Rag

Music by Scott Joplin

Trio

The Night We Called It A Day

Words by Tom Adair
Music by Matt Dennis

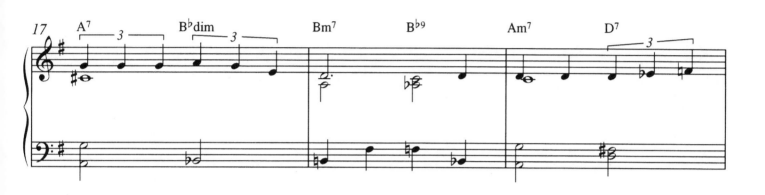

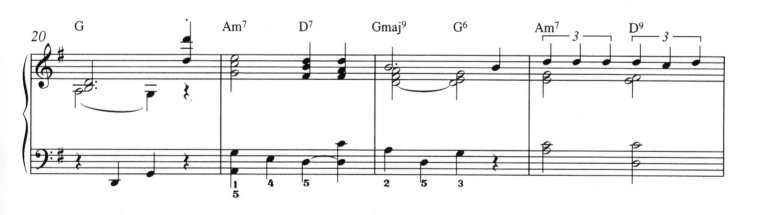

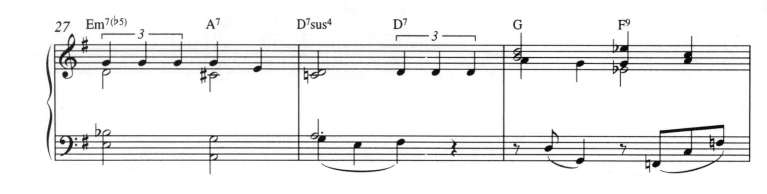

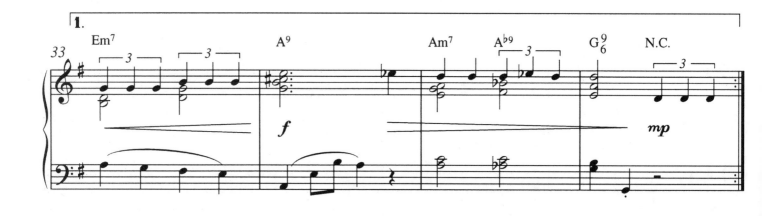

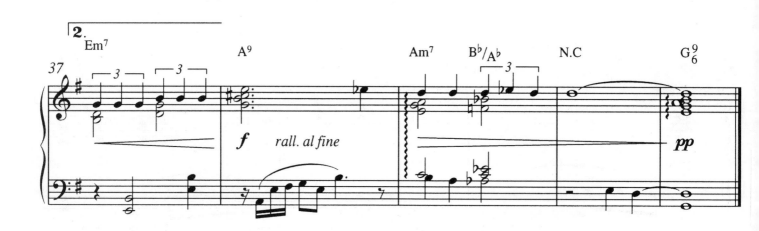

So What

Music by Miles Davis

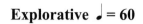

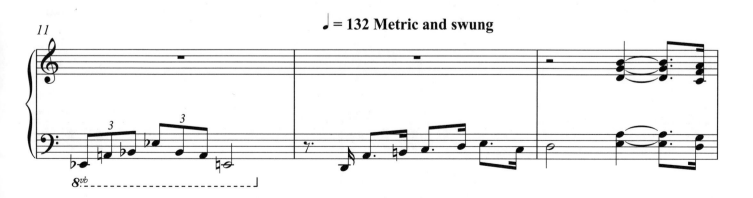

125

Wade In The Water

Traditional, Arranged by Ramsey Lewis

Repeat ad lib., using chord sequence -

D⁷

G⁷

128

Being Alive
(from the musical play "Company")

Words & Music by Stephen Sondheim

Moderato (with a beat)

Do-Re-Mi

(from the musical "The Sound Of Music")

Words by Oscar Hammerstein II & Music by Richard Rodgers

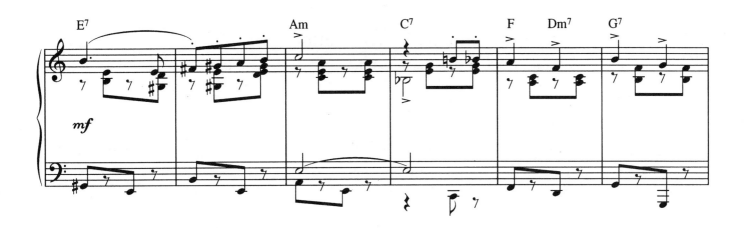

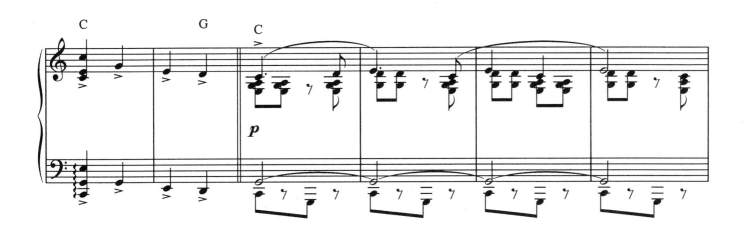

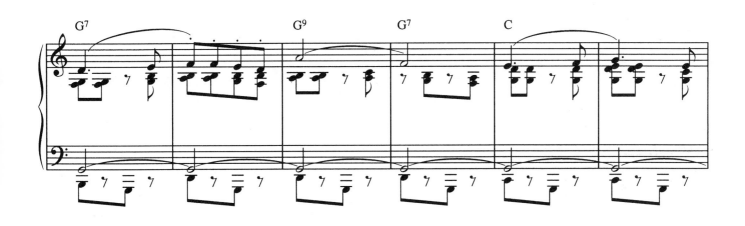

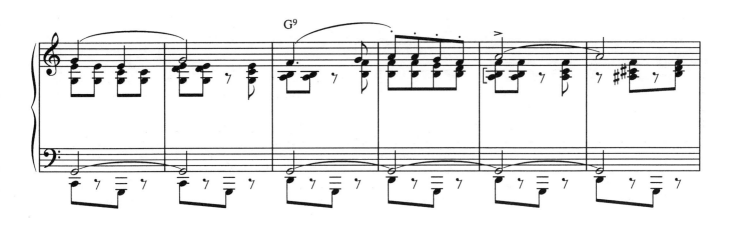

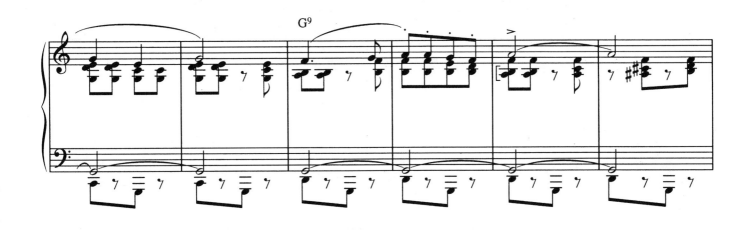

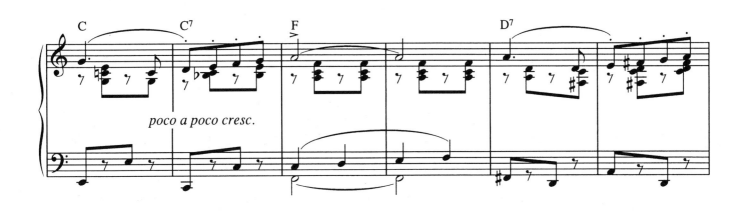

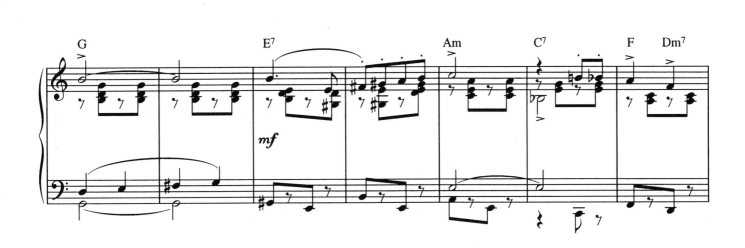

Diamonds Are A Girl's Best Friend

(from the musical film "Gentlemen Prefer Blondes")

Words by Leo Robin
Music by Jule Styne

Now That I've Seen Her

(from the musical "Miss Saigon")

Words by Alain Boublil & Richard Maltby Jr.
Music by Claude-Michel Schönberg

140

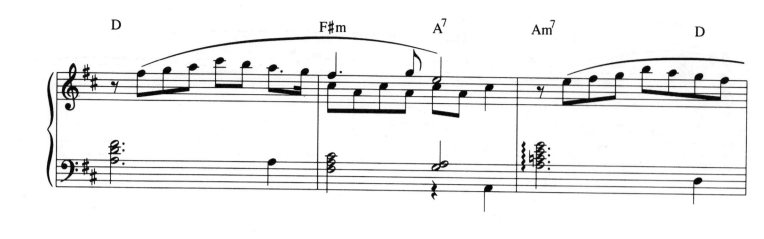

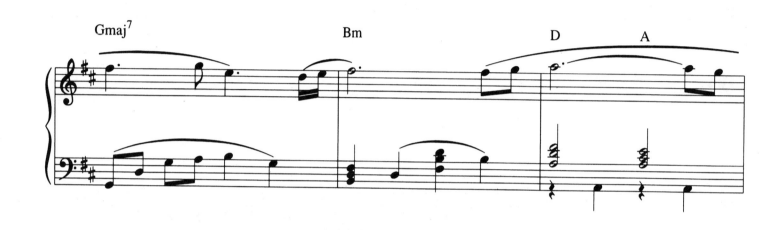

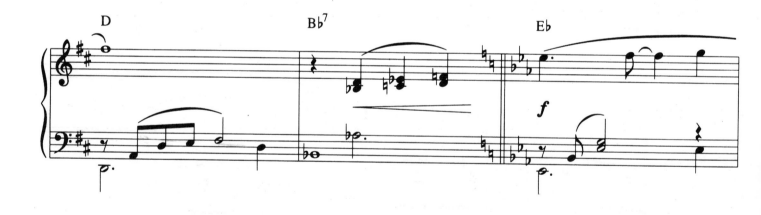

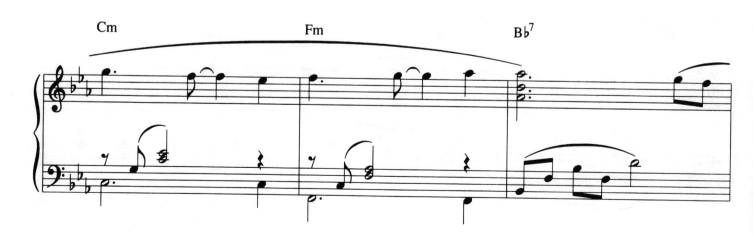

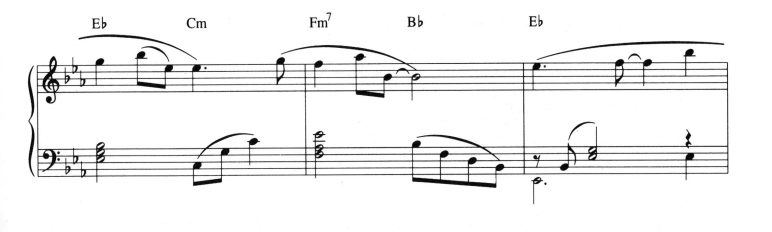

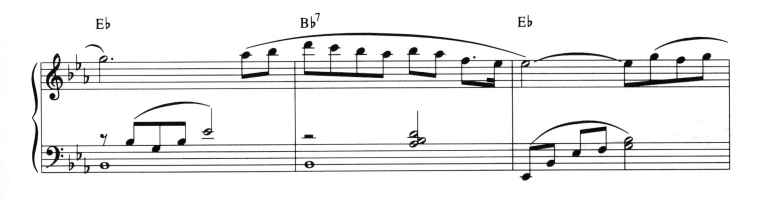

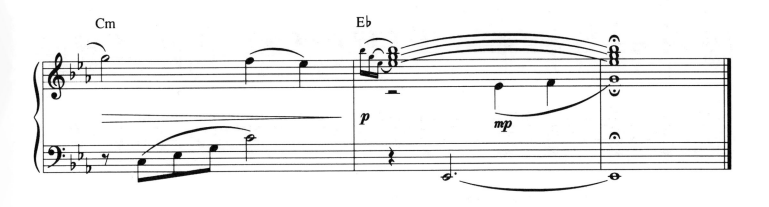

Maybe This Time
(from the musical "Cabaret")

Words by Fred Ebb
Music by John Kander

Slowly with expression

145

Take That Look Off Your Face
(from the musical "Tell Me On A Sunday")

Words by Don Black
Music by Andrew Lloyd Webber

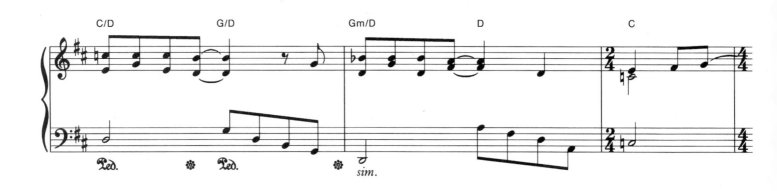

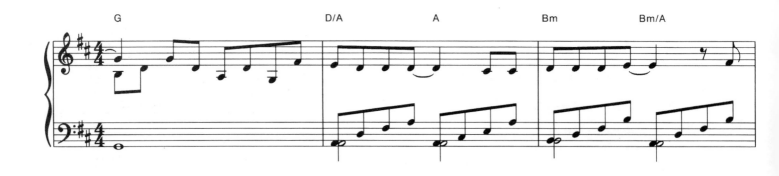

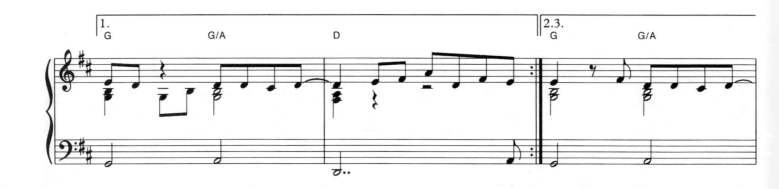

149

With One Look
(from the musical "Sunset Boulevard")

Words by Don Black & Christopher Hampton
Music by Andrew Lloyd Webber

Till There Was You

(from the musical "The Music Man")

Words & Music by Meredith Willson

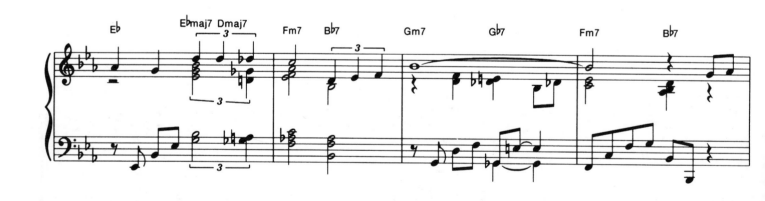

You'll Never Walk Alone
(from the musical "Carousel")

Words by Oscar Hammerstein II
Music by Richard Rodgers

Moderately